PROMISES
FOR LIFE

Ellie Claire
gift & paper expressions

...inspired by life

PROMISES
FOR LIFE

A LIFE WORTHWHILE

*W*hat makes life worthwhile is having a big enough objective,
something which catches our imagination and lays
hold of our allegiance.... What higher, more exalted,
and more compelling goal can there be than to know God?

J. I. Packer

*T*here are four steps to accomplishment:
Plan Purposefully.
Prepare Prayerfully.
Proceed Positively.
Pursue Persistently.

*T*he purpose of life is a life of purpose.

Robert Byrne

> Lord, Your love reaches to the heavens, Your loyalty
> to the skies. Your goodness is as high as the mountains.
> Your justice is as deep as the great ocean.
>
> PSALM 36:5-6 NCV

A LIFE WORTHWHILE

HOW HIGH OUR DREAMS CAN SOAR

*G*od's gifts put man's best dreams to shame.

Elizabeth Barrett Browning

*M*ore things are wrought by prayer
Than this world dreams of.

Alfred, Lord Tennyson

*W*ith God's power working in us, God can do much, much more
than anything we can ask or imagine.

Ephesians 3:20 NCV

*T*here is a past which is gone forever, but there is
a future which is still our own.

Frederick William Robertson

The stars exist that we might know how high
our dreams can soar.

HOW HIGH OUR
DREAMS CAN SOAR

_____

_____

_____

_____

_____

_____

_____

_____

_____

_____

_____

_____

_____

_____

_____

_____

_____

_____

SPECIAL PLANS

*T*his is the real gift: you have been given the breath of life,
designed with a unique, one-of-a-kind soul that exists forever—
the way that you choose to live it doesn't change the fact
that you've been given the gift of being now and forever.
Priceless in value, you are handcrafted by God,
who has a personal design and plan for each of us.

*M*ay God's love guide you through the special plans
He has for your life.

*A*llow your dreams a place in your prayers and plans.
God-given dreams can help you move into the
future He is preparing for you.

**The Lord will work out His plans for my life—
for Your faithful love, O Lord, endures forever.**

PSALM 138:8 NLT

SPECIAL PLANS

_____

_____

_____

_____

_____

_____

_____

_____

_____

_____

_____

_____

_____

_____

_____

_____

_____

_____

THE REASON FOR THE JOURNEY

*Don't walk in front of me—
I may not follow.
Don't walk behind me—
I may not lead.
Walk beside me—
And just be my friend.*

*I cry out to God Most High, to God who will
fulfill His purpose for me.*

Psalm 57:2 NLT

*Two roads diverged in a wood, and I—
I took the one less traveled by,
And that has made all the difference.*

Robert Lee Frost

We may run, walk, stumble, drive, or fly, but let us
never lose sight of the reason for the journey or
miss a chance to see a rainbow on the way.

GLORIA GAITHER

THE REASON FOR
THE JOURNEY

WONDERFUL LOVE

Show the wonder of Your great love.... Keep me as the apple
of Your eye; hide me in the shadow of Your wings.

Psalm 17:7-8 NIV

Give thanks to the Lord, for He is good!
His faithful love endures forever.

Psalm 136:1 NLT

The Lord is kind and shows mercy.
He does not become angry quickly but
is full of love.
The Lord is good to everyone;
He is merciful to all He has made.
Lord, everything You have made will praise You;
those who belong to You will bless You.
They will tell about the glory of Your kingdom
and will speak about Your power.
Then everyone will know the mighty things You do.

Psalm 145:8-12 NCV

Every one of us as human beings is known and loved by the
Creator apart from every other human on earth.

JAMES DOBSON

WONDERFUL LOVE

SIMPLE THINGS

I still find each day too short for all the thoughts I want to think,
all the walks I want to take, all the books I want to read,
and all the friends I want to see. The longer I live, the more my
mind dwells upon the beauty and the wonder of the world.

John Burroughs

*G*od is the One who gives seed to the farmer and bread for food.
He will give you all the seed you need and make it grow so
there will be a great harvest from your goodness. He will make
you rich in every way so that you can always give freely.
And your giving through us will cause many to give thanks
to God. This service you do not only helps the needs of God's
people, it also brings many more thanks to God.

2 Corinthians 9:10–12 NCV

Joys come from simple and natural things: mists over meadows,
sunlight on leaves, the path of the moon over water.

SIGURD F. OLSON

SIMPLE THINGS

CHILD OF GOD

When we call on God, He bends down His ear to listen,
as a father bends down to listen to his little child.

Elizabeth Charles

He only is the Maker
of all things near and far;
He paints the wayside flower,
He lights the evening star;
the wind and waves obey Him,
by Him the birds are fed;
much more to us, His children,
He gives our daily bread.

Matthias Claudius

Remember you are very special to God as His
precious child. He has promised to complete the
good work He has begun in you. As you continue to
grow in Him, He will make you a blessing to others.

How great is the love the Father has lavished on us, that we
should be called children of God! And that is what we are!

1 JOHN 3:1 NIV

CHILD OF GOD

_____

_____

_____

_____

_____

_____

_____

_____

_____

_____

_____

_____

_____

_____

_____

_____

_____

_____

_____

SUCCESS IS...

Success is failure turned inside out,
The silver tint of the clouds of doubt,
And you never can tell how close you are,
It may be near when it seems so far.
So stick to the fight when you're hardest hit,
It's when things seem worst,
That you must not quit.

Success...is to spring to meet the day with a thrill at being alive.
It is to go forth to meet the morning in an ecstasy of joy.

Lillian Whiting

Success is neither fame, wealth, nor power; rather it is seeking,
knowing, loving, and obeying God. If you seek, you will know;
if you know, you will love; if you love, you will obey.

Charles Malik

It is not that we think we can do anything of lasting value
by ourselves. Our only power and success come from God.

2 CORINTHIANS 3:5 NLT

SUCCESS IS...

_____

_____

_____

_____

_____

_____

_____

_____

_____

_____

_____

_____

_____

_____

_____

_____

_____

_____

_____

FAMILY TIES

There's no vocabulary
For love within a family, love that's lived in
But not looked at, love within the light of which
All else is seen, the love within which
All other love finds speech.

T. S. Eliot

Happiness is being at peace, being with loved ones, being
comfortable... But most of all, it's having those loved ones.

Johnny Cash

As for me and my family, we will serve the Lord.

Joshua 24:15 NLT

When you look at your life, the greatest happinesses
are family happinesses.

Joyce Brothers

I know of no realm of life that can provide more companionship
in a lonely world or greater feelings of security and purpose
in chaotic times than the close ties of a family.

CHARLES R. SWINDOLL

FAMILY TIES

SECRET OF ABUNDANT LIFE

To love by freely giving is its own reward.
To be possessed by love and to in turn give love away
is to find the secret of abundant life.

Gloria Gaither

I have come that they may have life, and that they
may have it more abundantly.

John 10:10 NKJV

There are only two ways to live your life.
One is as though nothing is a miracle.
The other is as though everything is a miracle.

Richard Crashaw

God made you so you could share in His creation,
could love and laugh and know Him.

Ted Griffen

Not what we have but what we enjoy
constitutes our abundance.

JOHN PETIT-SENN

SECRET OF ABUNDANT LIFE

SPECIAL GIFTS

Every person ever created is so special that their presence in the world makes it richer and fuller and more wonderful than it could ever have been without them.

We were not sent into this world to do anything into which we cannot put our hearts.

John Ruskin

Use what talents you possess: the woods would be very silent if no birds sang there except those that sang best.

Henry van Dyke

God gives everyone a special gift and a special place to use it.

Where you are right now is God's place for you. Live and obey and love and believe right there.

1 CORINTHIANS 7:17 THE MESSAGE

SPECIAL GIFTS

LOVE ONE ANOTHER

*W*atch what God does, and then you do it, like children who learn proper behavior from their parents. Mostly what God does is love you. Keep company with Him and learn a life of love. Observe how Christ loved us. His love was not cautious but extravagant. He didn't love in order to get something from us but to give everything of Himself to us. Love like that.

Ephesians 5:1-2 THE MESSAGE

I pray that your love for each other will overflow more and more, and that you will keep on growing in your knowledge and understanding.

Philippians 1:9 NLT

Getting things accomplished isn't nearly as important as taking time for love.

JANETTE OKE

LOVE ONE ANOTHER

_____

_____

_____

_____

_____

_____

_____

_____

_____

_____

_____

_____

_____

_____

_____

_____

_____

_____

GOD'S HEART

*T*he Lord your God is with you....
He will take great delight in you,
He will quiet you with His love,
He will rejoice over you with singing.

Zephaniah 3:17 NIV

*T*here is no need to plead that the love of God shall
fill our hearts as though He were unwilling to fill us....
Love is pressing around us on all sides like air.
Cease to resist it and instantly love takes possession.

Amy Carmichael

God's heart is the most sensitive and tender of all. No act
goes unnoticed, no matter how insignificant or small.

RICHARD J. FOSTER

GOD'S HEART

_____

_____

_____

_____

_____

_____

_____

_____

_____

_____

_____

_____

_____

_____

_____

_____

_____

A SMILE COSTS NOTHING

A smile is a curve that sets everything straight.

Phyllis Diller

*T*he thing that goest farthest towards making life worth while,
That costs the least, and does the most, is just a pleasant smile....
It's full of worth and goodness too, with manly kindness blent,
It's worth a million dollars and it doesn't cost a cent.

Wilbur D. Nesbit

A smile is a light in the window of the soul indicating
that the heart is at home.

A happy heart makes the face cheerful.

Proverbs 15:13 NIV

A smile costs nothing but gives much. It takes but a moment,
and the memory of it sometimes lasts forever.

A SMILE COSTS NOTHING

GOD WILL BE MY GUIDE

We do not understand the intricate pattern of the stars in their courses, but we know that He who created them does, and that just as surely as He guides them, He is charting a safe course for us.

Billy Graham

To be glad of life, because it gives you the chance to love and to work and to play and to look up at the stars; to be satisfied with your possessions, but not contented with yourself until you have made the best of them;...to think seldom of your enemies, often of your friends, and every day of Christ; and to spend as much time as you can, with body and with spirit in God's out-of-doors—these are little guideposts on the footpath to peace.

Henry van Dyke

God shall be my hope, my stay, my guide and lantern to my feet.

William Shakespeare

But I'll take the hand of those who don't know the way, who can't see where they're going. I'll be a personal guide to them, directing them through unknown country.

ISAIAH 42:16 THE MESSAGE

GOD WILL BE MY GUIDE

_____

_____

_____

_____

_____

_____

_____

_____

_____

_____

_____

_____

_____

_____

_____

_____

A WORK OF ART

*E*ach one of us is God's special work of art. Through us, He teaches and inspires, delights and encourages, informs and uplifts all those who view our lives. God, the master artist, is most concerned about expressing Himself—His thoughts and His intentions—through what He paints in our character.... [He] wants to paint a beautiful portrait of His Son in and through your life. A painting like no other in all of time.

Joni Eareckson Tada

*W*hether we are poets or parents or teachers or artists or gardeners, we must start where we are and use what we have. In the process of creation and relationship, what seems mundane and trivial may show itself to be holy, precious, part of a pattern.

Luci Shaw

I will give thanks to You, for I am fearfully and wonderfully made; wonderful are Your works.

PSALM 139:14 NASB

A WORK OF ART

ENFOLDED IN PEACE

I will let God's peace infuse every part of today. As the chaos swirls and life's demands pull at me on all sides, I will breathe in God's peace that surpasses all understanding. He has promised that He would set within me a peace too deeply planted to be affected by unexpected or exhausting demands.

*C*alm me, O Lord, as You stilled the storm,
Still me, O Lord, keep me from harm.
Let all the tumult within me cease,
Enfold me, Lord, in Your peace.

Celtic Traditional

*G*od cannot give us a happiness and peace apart from Himself, because it is not there. There is no such thing.

C. S. Lewis

Don't worry about anything; instead, pray about everything. Tell God what you need, and thank Him for all He has done. Then you will experience God's peace, which exceeds anything we can understand. His peace will guard your hearts and minds as you live in Christ Jesus.

PHILIPPIANS 4:7 NLT

ENFOLDED IN PEACE

_____
_____
_____
_____
_____
_____
_____
_____
_____
_____
_____
_____
_____
_____
_____
_____
_____
_____
_____
_____

EVERYDAY IS A GIFT TO CHERISH

*E*verything in life is most fundamentally a gift.
And you receive it best, and you live it best,
by holding it with very open hands.

Leo O'Donovan

*G*o after a life of love as if your life depended on it—
because it does. Give yourselves to the gifts God gives you.
Most of all, try to proclaim His truth.

1 Corinthians 14:1 THE MESSAGE

*E*very day we live is a priceless gift of God, loaded with
possibilities to learn something new, to gain fresh insights.

Dale Evans Rogers

**Time is a very precious gift of God; so precious
that it's only given to us moment by moment.**

AMELIA BARR

EVERYDAY IS A GIFT
TO CHERISH

LIVING TOGETHER

*M*other had a thousand thoughts to get through within a day, and...most of these were about avoiding disaster.

Natalie Kusz

A family is a unit composed not only of children but of men, women, an occasional animal, and the common cold.

Ogden Nash

*Y*ou're blessed when you can show people how to cooperate instead of compete or fight. That's when you discover who you really are, and your place in God's family.

Matthew 5:9 THE MESSAGE

Family life is too intimate to be preserved by the spirit of justice. It can be sustained by a spirit of love which goes beyond justice.

REINHOLD NIEBUHR

LIVING TOGETHER

_____

_____

_____

_____

_____

_____

_____

_____

_____

_____

_____

_____

_____

_____

_____

_____

_____

RESTORATION

*T*he Spirit of the Sovereign Lord is upon me,
for the Lord has anointed me
to bring good news to the poor.
He has sent me to comfort the brokenhearted
and to proclaim that captives will be released
and prisoners will be freed.
He has sent me to tell those who mourn
that the time of the Lord's favor has come,
and with it, the day of God's anger against their enemies.
To all who mourn in Israel,
He will give a crown of beauty for ashes,
a joyous blessing instead of mourning,
festive praise instead of despair.
In their righteousness, they will be like great oaks
that the Lord has planted for His own glory.

Isaiah 61:1-3 NLT

The Lord promises to bind up the brokenhearted,
to give relief and full deliverance to those whose
spirits have been weighed down.

CHARLES R. SWINDOLL

RESTORATION

_____

_____

_____

_____

_____

_____

_____

_____

_____

_____

_____

_____

_____

_____

_____

_____

_____

_____

TO REACH A DESTINATION

*T*here's no thrill in easy sailing
when the skies are clear and blue,
There's no joy in merely doing things
which anyone can do.
But there is some satisfaction
that is mighty sweet to take,
when you reach a destination
that you thought you'd never make.

Spirella

*D*estiny is not a matter of chance, it is a matter of choice.
It is not a thing to be waited for; it is a thing to be achieved.

William Jennings Bryan

But now you have arrived at your destination: By faith
in Christ you are in direct relationship with God.

GALATIANS 3:25-26 THE MESSAGE

TO REACH A
DESTINATION

_____

_____

_____

_____

_____

_____

_____

_____

_____

_____

_____

_____

_____

_____

_____

BLESSINGS AWAIT

*H*aving someone who understands is a great blessing for ourselves. Being someone who understands is a great blessing to others.

Janette Oke

*L*ift up your eyes. Your heavenly Father waits to bless you— in inconceivable ways to make your life what you never dreamed it could be.

Anne Ortlund

*A*nd God can give you more blessings than you need. Then you will always have plenty of everything— enough to give to every good work.

2 Corinthians 9:8 NCV

Some blessings—like rainbows after rain or a friend's listening ear—are extraordinary gifts waiting to be discovered in an ordinary day.

BLESSINGS AWAIT

A SPLENDID GIFT

*T*his bright, new day, complete with twenty-four hours of opportunities, choices, and attitudes comes with a perfectly matched set of 1,440 minutes. This unique gift, this one day, cannot be exchanged, replaced or refunded. Handle with care. Make the most of it. There is only one to a customer!

*Y*ou have a unique message to deliver, a unique song to sing, a unique act of love to bestow. This message, this song, and this act of love have been entrusted exclusively to the one and only you.

John Powell

*I*sn't everything you have and everything you are sheer gifts from God?

1 Corinthians 4:7 THE MESSAGE

Live your life while you have it. Life is a splendid gift—there is nothing small about it.

FLORENCE NIGHTINGALE

A SPLENDID GIFT

_____

_____

_____

_____

_____

_____

_____

_____

_____

_____

_____

_____

_____

_____

_____

_____

_____

_____

THE ABSURDITIES
OF THE DAY

*F*inish each day and be done with it. You have done what you could; some blunders and absurdities have crept in; forget them as soon as you can. Tomorrow is a new day; you shall begin it serenely and with too high a spirit to be encumbered with your old nonsense. This day is all that is good and fair. It is too dear, with its hopes and invitations, to waste a moment on yesterdays.

Ralph Waldo Emerson

*W*e ought to be able to learn things secondhand. There is not enough time for us to make all the mistakes ourselves.

Harriet Hall

Encourage one another daily,
as long as it is called Today.

HEBREWS 3:13 NIV

THE ABSURDITIES OF THE DAY

DEAR GOD...

You are a child of your heavenly Father. Confide in Him. Your faith in His love and power can never be bold enough.

Basilea Schlink

*W*here are you? Start there. Openly and freely declare your need to the One who cares deeply.

Charles R. Swindoll

*W*e must take our troubles to the Lord, but we must do more than that; we must leave them there.

Hannah Whitall Smith

*E*mbrace this God-life. Really embrace it, and nothing will be too much for you.... That's why I urge you to pray for absolutely everything, ranging from small to large. Include everything as you embrace this God-life, and you'll get God's everything.

Mark 11:22-24 THE MESSAGE

You pay God a compliment by asking great things of Him.

TERESA OF AVILA

DEAR GOD...

_____

_____

_____

_____

_____

_____

_____

_____

_____

_____

_____

_____

_____

_____

_____

_____

_____

_____

_____

DESIGNED ON PURPOSE

*I*t's in Christ that we find out who we are and what we are living
for. Long before we first heard of Christ and got our hopes up,
He had His eye on us, had designs on us for glorious living, part of
the overall purpose He is working out in everything and everyone.

Ephesians 1:11-12 THE MESSAGE

*T*o every thing there is a season,
A time for every purpose under the heaven.

Ecclesiastes 3:1 NKJV

*A*ll the days ordained for me were written in Your book
before one of them came to be.

Psalm 139:16 NIV

I delight to do Your will, O my God.

Psalm 40:8 NKJV

The patterns of our days are always rearranging...
and each design for living is unique,
graced with its own special beauty.

DESIGNED ON PURPOSE

_____

_____

_____

_____

_____

_____

_____

_____

_____

_____

_____

_____

_____

_____

_____

TREASURE TODAY

See each morning a world made anew, as if it were
the morning of the very first day;...treasure and use it,
as if it were the final hour of the very last day.

Fay Hartzell Arnold

For the Lord grants wisdom!
From His mouth come knowledge and understanding.
He grants a treasure of common sense to the honest.
He is a shield to those who walk with integrity.
He guards the paths of the just
and protects those who are faithful to Him.
Then you will understand what is right, just, and fair,
and you will find the right way to go.

Proverbs 2:5-9 nlt

In ordinary life we hardly realize that we
receive a great deal more than we give, and that it
is only with gratitude that life becomes rich.

Dietrich Bonhoeffer

Normal day, let me be aware of the treasure you are. Let me
learn from you, love you, bless you before you depart. Let me
not pass you by in quest of some rare and perfect tomorrow.

TREASURE TODAY

IN THE FINAL ANALYSIS

If you are successful, you will win some
false friends and some true enemies;
Succeed anyway.
If you are honest and frank,
people may cheat you;
Be honest and frank anyway....
You see, in the final analysis,
it is between you and God;
it was never between you
and them anyway.

What you spend years building,
someone could destroy overnight;
Build anyway.
If you find serenity and happiness,
they may be jealous;
Be happy anyway....
You see, in the final analysis,
it is between you and God;
it was never between you
and them anyway.

Mother Teresa

Keep us forgiven with You and forgiving others.

MATTHEW 6:12 THE MESSAGE

IN THE FINAL ANALYSIS

GOD HEARS

*W*e can now come fearlessly into God's presence,
assured of His glad welcome.

Ephesians 3:12 NLT

I love those who love Me;
And those who diligently seek Me will find Me.
Riches and honor are with Me,
Enduring wealth and righteousness.
My fruit is better than gold, even pure gold,
And my yield better than choicest silver.

Proverbs 8:17-19 NASB

*O*ne single grateful thought raised to heaven
is the most perfect prayer.

G. E. Lessing

No matter where we are, God can hear us from there!

GOD HEARS

SEEK FIRST

Why do you worry about clothes? Look at how the lilies in the field grow. They don't work or make clothes for themselves. But I tell you that even Solomon with his riches was not dressed as beautifully as one of these flowers. God clothes the grass in the field, which is alive today but tomorrow is thrown into the fire. So you can be even more sure that God will clothe you. Don't have so little faith! Don't worry and say, "What will we eat?" or "What will we drink?" or "What will we wear?" The people who don't know God keep trying to get these things, and your Father in heaven knows you need them. Seek first God's kingdom and what God wants. Then all your other needs will be met as well.

Matthew 6:28–33 NCV

Trust the past to the mercy of God, the present
to His love, and the future to His Providence.

AUGUSTINE

SEEK FIRST

_____
_____
_____
_____
_____
_____
_____
_____
_____
_____
_____
_____
_____
_____
_____
_____
_____
_____

A FEELING THAT NURTURES THE SOUL

*C*an you see the holiness in those things you take for granted—
a paved road or a washing machine? If you concentrate on finding
what is good in every situation, you will discover that your life will
suddenly be filled with gratitude, a feeling that nurtures the soul.

Harold Kushner

*I*t is good to give thanks to the Lord
And to sing praises to Your name, O Most High;
To declare Your lovingkindness in the morning
And Your faithfulness by night.

Psalm 92:1-2 NASB

*G*ratitude. More aware of what you have than what
you don't. Recognizing the treasure in the simple—
a child's hug, fertile soil, a golden sunset.
Relishing in the comfort of the common—
a warm bed, a hot meal, a clean shirt.

Max Lucado

Gratitude is not only the greatest of virtues,
but the parent of all others.

CICERO

A FEELING THAT NURTURES THE SOUL

FORGIVENESS IS THE ANSWER

*L*ive creatively, friends. If someone falls into sin, forgivingly
restore him, saving your critical comments for yourself.
You might be needing forgiveness before the day's out.
Stoop down and reach out to those who are oppressed.
Share their burdens, and so complete Christ's law.

Galatians 6:1-3 THE MESSAGE

*F*orgiveness is the answer to the child's dream
of a miracle by which what is broken is made
whole again, what is soiled is again made clean.

Dag Hammarskjold

Love has been called the most effective motivational force in
all the world. When love is at work in us, it is remarkable how
giving and forgiving, understanding and tolerant we can be.

CHARLES R. SWINDOLL

FORGIVENESS IS
THE ANSWER

FEAR NOT

*D*on't be afraid, I've redeemed you. I've called your name.
You're mine. When you're in over your head, I'll be there
with you. When you're in rough waters, you will not go down.
When you're between a rock and a hard place, it won't be a
dead end—Because I am God, your personal God, The Holy
of Israel, your Savior. I paid a huge price for you...! *That's* how
much you mean to Me! *That's* how much I love you!

Isaiah 43:1–4 THE MESSAGE

*I*f God is for us, who is against us? He who did not spare
His own Son, but delivered Him over for us all,
how will He not also with Him freely give us all things?

Romans 8:31–32 NASB

Do not be afraid to enter the cloud that is
settling down on your life. God is in it.
The other side is radiant with His glory.

L. B. COWMAN

FEAR NOT

IN GOD'S DESIGN

God has designs on our future...and He has designed
us for the future. He has given us something to do
in the future that no one else can do.

Ruth Senter

Your life is a journey you must travel with a deep
consciousness of God. It cost God plenty to get you out of that
dead-end, empty-headed life you grew up in. He paid with Christ's
sacred blood, you know... It's because of this sacrificed Messiah...
that you trust God, that you know you have a future in God.

1 Peter 1:18-21 THE MESSAGE

God wants to continually add to us, to develop
and enlarge us—always building on what
He has already taught and built in us.

Never be afraid to trust an unknown future to a known God.

CORRIE TEN BOOM

IN GOD'S DESIGN

STILL I AM ONE

I am only one,
But still I am one.
I cannot do everything,
But still I can do something;
And because I cannot do everything
I will not refuse to do the something I can do.

Edward Everett Hale

A span of life is nothing. But the man or woman who
lives that span, they are something. They can fill that
tiny span with meaning, so its quality is immeasurable,
though its quantity may be insignificant.

Chaim Potok

*D*o all the good you can, and make as little fuss
about it as possible.

Charles Dickens

Anything is possible if a person believes.

MARK 9:23 NLT

STILL I AM ONE

_____

_____

_____

_____

_____

_____

_____

_____

_____

_____

_____

_____

_____

_____

_____

_____

_____

_____

_____

SHARE THE SECRET

*K*now that I'm on your side, right alongside you.
You're not in this alone. I want you woven into a tapestry
of love, in touch with everything there is to know of God.
Then you will have minds confident and at rest, focused on Christ,
God's great mystery. All the richest treasures of wisdom and
knowledge are embedded in that mystery and nowhere else.

Colossians 2:1-2 THE MESSAGE

*T*he real secret of happiness is not what you give or
what you receive, it's what you share.

*T*o be able to find joy in another's joy,
that is the secret of happiness.

**The secret of life is that all we have and are
is a gift of grace to be shared.**

LLOYD JOHN OGILVIE

SHARE THE SECRET

_____

_____

_____

_____

_____

_____

_____

_____

_____

_____

_____

_____

_____

_____

_____

_____

_____

COMPLETELY LOVED

*Y*ou are valuable just because you exist. Not because of what you do or what you have done, but simply because you are. Just think about the way Jesus honors you...and smile.

Max Lucado

*W*e are of such value to God that He came to live among us... and to guide us home. He will go to any length to seek us.... We can only respond by loving God for His love.

Catherine of Siena

*W*hat good news! God knows me completely and still loves me.

We love Him because He first loved us.

1 JOHN 4:19 NKJV

COMPLETELY LOVED

UNCONDITIONAL LOVE

*T*here is nothing we can do that will make God love us less, and there's nothing we can do that will make Him love us more. He will always and forever love us unconditionally. What He wants from us is that we love Him back with all our heart.

*D*o not dwell upon your inner failings…. Just do this: Bring your soul to the Great Physician—exactly as you are, even and especially at your worst moment…. For it is in such moments that you will most readily sense His healing presence.

Teresa of Avila

My grace is sufficient for you, for My strength is made perfect in weakness.

2 CORINTHIANS 12:9 NKJV

UNCONDITIONAL LOVE

GOD KNOWS YOU

*G*od knows everything about us. And He cares about
everything. Moreover, He can manage every situation.
And He loves us! Surely this is enough to open the wellsprings
of joy.... And joy is always a source of strength.

Hannah Whitall Smith

O Lord, You have examined my heart
and know everything about me.
You know when I sit down or stand up.
You know my thoughts even when I'm far away.
You see me when I travel
and when I rest at home.
You know everything I do.
You know what I am going to say....
You go before me and follow me.
You place Your hand of blessing on my head.

Psalm 139:1-5 NLT

God created the universe, but He also created you.
God knows you, God loves you, and God cares about
the tiniest details of your life.

BRUCE BICKEL AND STAN JANTZ

GOD KNOWS YOU

_____

_____

_____

_____

_____

_____

_____

_____

_____

_____

_____

_____

_____

_____

_____

_____

_____

_____

A LIFE OF PURPOSE

*H*appiness is living by inner purpose, not by outer pressures.

David Augsberger

I believe that nothing that happens to me is meaningless,
and that it is good for us all that it should be so, even if
it runs counter to our own wishes. As I see it, I'm here
for some purpose, and I only hope I may fulfill it.

Dietrich Bonhoeffer

*T*he meaning of earthly existence lies, not as we have grown used
to thinking, in prospering, but in the development of the soul.

Aleksandr Solzhenitsyn

> And we know that all things work together for
> good to those who love God, to those who are the
> called according to His purpose.
>
> ROMANS 8:28 NKJV

A LIFE OF PURPOSE

THINGS TO REMEMBER

*T*welve things to remember—
1) The value of time. 2) The success of perseverance.
3) The pleasure of working. 4) The dignity of simplicity.
5) The worth of character. 6) The power of kindness.
7) The influence of example. 8) The obligation of duty.
9) The wisdom of economy. 10) The virtue of patience.
11) The improvement of talent. 12) The joy of origination.

Marshall Field

*R*emember that fear always lurks behind perfectionism....
Confronting your fears and allowing yourself the right
to be human can, paradoxically, make you a far happier
and more productive person.

David M. Burns

*S*tep with care and great tact
And remember that life's a Great Balancing Act
Just never forget to be dexterous and deft
And never mix up your right foot with your left.

Dr. Seuss

Remember that the Lord will give you an
inheritance as your reward.

COLOSSIANS 3:24 NLT

THINGS TO REMEMBER

_____

_____

_____

_____

_____

_____

_____

_____

_____

_____

_____

_____

_____

_____

_____

_____

_____

ONE BIG HAPPY FAMILY

*F*amily faces are magic mirrors. Looking at people who belong to us, we see the past, present, and future.

Gail Lumet Buckley

*L*et us not become weary in doing good, for at the proper time we will reap a harvest if we do not give up. Therefore, as we have opportunity, let us do good to all people, especially to those who belong to the family of believers.

Galatians 6:9-10 NIV

*W*hat families have in common the world around is that they are the place where people learn who they are and how to be that way.

Jean Illsley Clarke

Call it clan, call it a network, call it a tribe, call it a family. Whatever you call it, whoever you are, you need one.

JANE HOWARD

ONE BIG HAPPY FAMILY

TRULY YOU

*E*verybody can be great. Because anybody can serve. You don't have to have a college degree to serve. You don't have to make your subject and your verb agree to serve.... You only need a heart full of grace. A soul generated by love.

Martin Luther King Jr.

*G*reatness lies not in being strong, but in the right use of strength.

Henry Ward Beecher

I pray that from His glorious, unlimited resources He will empower you with inner strength through His Spirit. Then Christ will make His home in your hearts as you trust in Him. Your roots will grow down into God's love and keep you strong.

Ephesians 3:16–17 NLT

What lies behind us and what lies before us are tiny matters compared to what lies within us.

RALPH WALDO EMERSON

TRULY YOU

_____

_____

_____

_____

_____

_____

_____

_____

_____

_____

_____

_____

_____

_____

_____

_____

_____

_____

_____

_____

WEAVE A BEAUTIFUL REALITY

If I'm not free to fail, I'm not free to take risks, and everything in life that's worth doing involves a willingness to take a risk.

Madeleine L'Engle

Let's practice real love. This is the only way we'll know we're living truly, living in God's reality. It's also the way to shut down debilitating self-criticism.... For God is greater than our worried hearts and knows more about us than we do ourselves. And friends, once that's taken care of and we're no longer accusing or condemning ourselves, we're bold and free before God!

1 John 3:18-21 THE MESSAGE

Do not think of today's failures but of the success that may come tomorrow.... Remember, no effort that we make to attain something beautiful is ever lost. Sometime, somewhere, somehow, we shall find that which we seek.

Helen Keller

The challenge of life is to take a single strand of
a dream and from it weave a beautiful reality.

WEAVE A BEAUTIFUL REALITY

_____

_____

_____

_____

_____

_____

_____

_____

_____

_____

_____

_____

_____

_____

_____

_____

HAPPINESS AND GRATITUDE

*O*ur inner happiness depends not on what we experience but on the degree of our gratitude to God, whatever the experience.

Albert Schweitzer

*E*xamine and see how good the Lord is. Happy is the person who trusts Him. You who belong to the Lord, fear Him! Those who fear Him will have everything they need.

Psalm 34:8-9 NCV

*L*ife is to be fortified by many friendships. To love, and be loved, is the greatest happiness of existence.

Sydney Smith

It is not how much we have, but how much
we enjoy, that makes happiness.

CHARLES H. SPURGEON

HAPPINESS AND GRATITUDE

_____

_____

_____

_____

_____

_____

_____

_____

_____

_____

_____

_____

_____

_____

_____

_____

HIS BEAUTIFUL WORLD

The God who holds the whole world in His hands wraps Himself in the splendor of the sun's light and walks among the clouds.

Forbid that I should walk through Thy beautiful world with unseeing eyes: Forbid that the lure of the market-place should ever entirely steal my heart away from the love of the open acres and the green trees: Forbid that under the low roof of workshop or office or study I should ever forget Thy great overarching sky.

John Baillie

The whole earth is full of His glory!

ISAIAH 6:3 NKJV

Our Creator would never have made such lovely days, and given us the deep hearts to enjoy them, above and beyond all thought, unless we were meant to be immortal.

NATHANIEL HAWTHORNE

HIS BEAUTIFUL WORLD

_____

_____

_____

_____

_____

_____

_____

_____

_____

_____

_____

_____

_____

_____

_____

_____

TOTALLY AWARE

*G*od is every moment totally aware of each one of us. Totally aware in intense concentration and love.... No one passes through any area of life, happy or tragic, without the attention of God.

Eugenia Price

*I*f you have a special need today, focus your full attention on the goodness and greatness of your Father rather than on the size of your need. Your need is so small compared to His ability to meet it.

May you have the power to understand,
as all God's people should, how wide, how long,
how high, and how deep His love is.

EPHESIANS 3:18 NLT

TOTALLY AWARE

THE MEASURE OF LEADERSHIP

They are the best leaders who most fully understand the nature of things...who possess an active, far ranging imagination which can see many possibilities; who have a sense of values, so that among possibilities they are able to choose the most excellent.

Arthur E. Morgan

The measure of leadership is the caliber of people who choose to follow you.

Dennis A. Peer

Never tell people how to do things. Tell them what to do, and they will surprise you with their ingenuity.

George S. Patton Jr.

But among you it should be quite different. Whoever wants to be a leader among you must be your servant.

MARK 10:43 NLT

THE MEASURE OF LEADERSHIP

MADE FOR JOY

*O*ur hearts were made for joy. Our hearts were made to enjoy the One who created them. Too deeply planted to be much affected by the ups and downs of life, this joy is a knowing and a being known by our Creator. He sets our hearts alight with radiant joy.

*I*f one is joyful, it means that one is faithfully living for God, and that nothing else counts; and if one gives joy to others one is doing God's work. With joy without and joy within, all is well.

Janet Erskine Stuart

*L*ive for today but hold your hands open to tomorrow. Anticipate the future and its changes with joy. There is a seed of God's love in every event, every circumstance, every unpleasant situation in which you may find yourself.

Barbara Johnson

The joy of the Lord is your strength.

NEHEMIAH 8:10 NKJV

MADE FOR JOY

CONTENTMENT

I have learned to be content in whatever circumstances I am.
I know how to get along with humble means, and I also know
how to live in prosperity; in any and every circumstance
I have learned the secret of being filled and going hungry,
both of having abundance and suffering need. I can do all
things through Him who strengthens me.

Philippians **4:11-13** NASB

Be content with who you are, and don't put on airs.
God's strong hand is on you; He'll promote you at the right time.
Live carefree before God; He is most careful with you.

1 Peter 5:6-7 THE MESSAGE

*G*odliness with contentment is great gain.
For we brought nothing into the world,
and we can take nothing out of it. But if we have
food and clothing, we will be content with that.

1 Timothy 6:6-8 NIV

Contentment is not the fulfillment of what you want,
but the realization of how much you already have.

CONTENTMENT

_____

_____

_____

_____

_____

_____

_____

_____

_____

_____

_____

_____

_____

_____

_____

_____

_____

ATTITUDE IS EVERYTHING

A positive attitude may not solve all your problems, but it will annoy enough people to make it worth the effort.

Herm Albright

*I*f you have any encouragement from being united with Christ, if any comfort from His love, if any fellowship with the Spirit, if any tenderness and compassion, then make my joy complete by being like-minded, having the same love, being one in spirit and purpose. Do nothing out of selfish ambition or vain conceit, but in humility consider others better than yourselves.

Philippians 2:1-3 NIV

*T*is easy enough to be pleasant,
When life flows along like a song;
But the man worthwhile is the one who will smile
When everything does dead wrong;
For the test of the heart is trouble,
And it always comes with the years,
But the smile that is worth the praise of earth
Is the smile that comes through tears.

Ella Wheeler Wilcox

A strong positive mental attitude will create
more miracles than any wonder drug.

PATRICIA NEAL

ATTITUDE IS EVERYTHING

ALWAYS THERE

God is always present in the temple of your heart...His home.
And when you come in to meet Him there, you find that it is
the one place of deep satisfaction where every longing is met.

Always be in a state of expectancy, and see that you
leave room for God to come in as He likes.

Oswald Chambers

How lovely are Your dwelling places, O Lord of hosts!
My soul longed and even yearned for the courts of the Lord;
my heart and my flesh sing for joy to the living God....
For a day in Your courts is better than a thousand outside.

Psalm 84:1-2, 10 NASB

We need never shout across the spaces to an absent God.
He is nearer than our own soul,
closer than our most secret thoughts.

A. W. TOZER

ALWAYS THERE

_____

_____

_____

_____

_____

_____

_____

_____

_____

_____

_____

_____

_____

_____

_____

_____

_____

AT THE DINNER TABLE

*T*he most remarkable thing about my mother is that for
thirty years she served the family nothing but leftovers.
The original meal has never been found.

Calvin Trillin

A mother is a person who, seeing there are only four pieces of pie
for five people, promptly announces she never did care for pie.

Tenneva Jordan

*K*eep on loving each other as brothers and sisters.
Remember to welcome strangers, because some who have
done this have welcomed angels without knowing it.

Hebrews 13:1-2 NCV

*M*an cannot live by bread alone; he needs peanut butter.

Barbara Johnson

The incredible gift of the ordinary! Glory comes
streaming from the table of daily life.

MACRINA WIEDERKEHR

AT THE DINNER TABLE

LIFE IS A SPECIAL OCCASION

I would rather be ashes than dust! I would rather that my spark would burn out in a brilliant blaze than it should be stifled by dry rot. I would rather be a superb meteor, every atom of me in magnificent glow, than a sleepy and permanent planet. The proper function of man is to live, not to exist. I shall not waste my days in trying to prolong them. I shall use my time.

Jack London

I can't tell you how much I long for you to enter this wide-open, spacious life.... Your lives aren't small, but you're living them in a small way. I'm speaking as plainly as I can and with great affection. Open up your lives. Live openly and expansively!

2 Corinthians 6:11-13 THE MESSAGE

Bottom line, wasn't life itself a special occasion?

JAN KARON

LIFE IS A SPECIAL OCCASION

_____

_____

_____

_____

_____

_____

_____

_____

_____

_____

_____

_____

_____

_____

_____

_____

TOWARD THE GOAL

We need to set goals for ourselves. Start today.... If you don't have any goals, make your first goal "getting some goals." You probably won't start living happily ever after, but you may start living happily, purposefully, and with gratitude.... Goals are gratitude in action. They give us the opportunity to build on what we already have. While achieving goals can be a lengthy process, we can learn to be grateful for each stage in the process of setting and meeting goals.

Melodie Beattie

A good goal is like a strenuous exercise—it makes you stretch.

Mary Kay Ash

Obstacles are those frightful things you see when you take your eyes off the goal.

Hannah More

I've got my eye on the goal, where God is beckoning us onward—to Jesus.

PHILIPPIANS 3:13 THE MESSAGE

TOWARD THE GOAL

THE ART OF COURAGE

Courage is doing what you're afraid to do.
There can be no courage unless you're scared.

Eddie Rickenbacker

Courage is the art of being the only one
who knows you're scared to death.

Harold Wilson

I wanted you to see what real courage is.... It's when
you know you're licked before you begin but you begin
anyway and you see it through no matter what.

Harper Lee

The only courage that matters is the kind that gets
you from one moment to the next.

Mignon McLaughlin

This is my command—be strong and courageous!
Do not be afraid or discouraged. For the Lord your God
is with you wherever you go.

JOSHUA 1:9 NLT

THE ART OF COURAGE

_____

_____

_____

_____

_____

_____

_____

_____

_____

_____

_____

_____

_____

_____

_____

_____

FAITH

Now faith is being sure of what we hope for and certain of what we do not see.... By faith we understand that the universe was formed at God's command, so that what is seen was not made out of what was visible.... And without faith it is impossible to please God, because anyone who comes to Him must believe that He exists and that He rewards those who earnestly seek Him.

Hebrews 11:1, 3, 6 NIV

Faith...means knowing something is real, this moment, all around you, even when you don't see it. Great faith isn't the ability to believe long and far into the misty future. It's simply taking God at His word and taking the next step.

JONI EARECKSON TADA

FAITH

FREE TO LIVE

God, your God, will cut away the thick calluses on your heart
and your children's hearts, freeing you to love God, your God,
with your whole heart and soul and live, really live.... And you
will make a new start, listening obediently to God, keeping all
His commandments that I'm commanding you today. God, your
God, will outdo Himself in making things go well for you....
Love God, your God. Walk in His ways. Keep His commandments,
regulations, and rules so that you will live, really live, live
exuberantly, blessed by God.... Love God, your God, listening
obediently to Him, firmly embracing Him. Oh yes, He is life itself.

Deuteronomy 30:6-9, 16, 20 THE MESSAGE

I asked God for all things that I might enjoy life.
He gave me life that I might enjoy all things.

FREE TO LIVE

THE GENEROUS SPIRIT

*Y*ou must give some time to your fellow men.
Even if it's a little thing, do something for others—something
for which you get no pay but the privilege of doing it.

Albert Schweitzer

*G*ive what you have. To someone,
it may be better than you dare to think.

Henry Wadsworth Longfellow

*W*hen you give a lunch or a dinner, don't invite only your friends,
your family, your other relatives, and your rich neighbors.
At another time they will invite you to eat with them, and you
will be repaid. Instead, when you give a feast, invite the poor,
the crippled, the lame, and the blind. Then you will be blessed,
because they have nothing and cannot pay you back.

Luke 14:12-14 NCV

*M*ake all you can, save all you can, give all you can.

John Wesley

We make a living by what we get,
we make a life by what we give.

SIR WINSTON CHURCHILL

THE GENEROUS SPIRIT

SOMEONE SPECIAL

The Creator thinks enough of you to have sent
Someone very special so that you might have life-abundantly,
joyfully, completely, and victoriously.

When we love someone, we want to be with them,
and we view their love for us with great honor even if they
are not a person of great status. For this reason—and not
because of our great status—God values our love.
So much, in fact, that He suffered greatly on our behalf.

John Chrysostom

One of Jesus' specialties is to make somebodies out of nobodies.

Henrietta Mears

God demonstrates His own love toward us, in that
while we were yet sinners, Christ died for us.

ROMANS 5:8 NASB

SOMEONE SPECIAL

_____

_____

_____

_____

_____

_____

_____

_____

_____

_____

_____

_____

_____

_____

_____

_____

_____

AN INSTRUMENT OF PEACE

*L*ord, Make me an instrument of Thy peace.
Where there is hatred, let me sow love;
Where there is injury, pardon;
Where there is doubt, faith;
Where there is despair, hope;
Where there is darkness, light;
Where there is sadness, joy....

Grant that I may not so much seek
to be consoled as to console,
to be understood as to understand,
to be loved as to love.

For it is in giving that we receive,
It is in pardoning that we are pardoned,
And it is in dying that we are born to eternal life.

Francis of Assisi

Peace I leave with you, My peace I give unto you....
Let not your heart be troubled, neither let it be afraid.

JOHN 14:27 NKJV

AN INSTRUMENT
OF PEACE

_____

_____

_____

_____

_____

_____

_____

_____

_____

_____

_____

_____

_____

_____

_____

_____

SETTLED IN SOLITUDE

*S*olitude liberates us from entanglements by carving out a space from which we can see ourselves and our situation before the Audience of One. Solitude provides the private place where we can take our bearings and so make God our North Star.

Os Guinness

*W*e must drink deeply from the very Source, the deep calm and peace of interior quietude and refreshment of God, allowing the pure water of divine grace to flow plentifully and unceasingly from the Source itself.

Mother Teresa

Whoever drinks of the water that I will give him shall never thirst; but the water that I will give him will become in him a well of water springing up to eternal life.

JOHN 4:13-14 NASB

SETTLED IN SOLITUDE

SLOW DOWN AND ENJOY LIFE

*S*low down and enjoy life. It's not only the scenery you miss by going too fast—you also miss the sense of where you are going and why.

Eddie Cantor

*D*ear friend, I pray that you may enjoy good health and that all may go well with you, even as your soul is getting along well.

3 John 1:2 NIV

*M*any persons have a wrong idea of what constitutes true happiness. It is not attained through self-gratification but through fidelity to a worthy purpose.

Helen Keller

Most folks are about as happy as they make up their minds to be.

ABRAHAM LINCOLN

SLOW DOWN AND ENJOY LIFE

LIVE SUCH A LIFE

*If we did the things we are capable of,
we would astound ourselves.*

Thomas Edison

*God has given us different gifts for doing certain things well....
If your gift is serving others, serve them well. If you are a
teacher, teach well. If your gift is to encourage others,
be encouraging. If it is giving, give generously. If God has
given you leadership ability, take the responsibility seriously.
And if you have a gift for showing kindness to others, do it gladly.*

Romans 12:6-8 NLT

*Start by doing what's necessary, then what's possible,
and suddenly you are doing the impossible.*

Francis of Assisi

*It's not your blue blood, your pedigree or your college
degree. It's what you do with your life that counts.*

Millard Fuller

Be such a person, and **live** such a life, that **if** every one
were such as you, and **every life** a life such as yours,
this earth would be God's paradise.

PHILLIPS BROOKS

LIVE SUCH A LIFE

DREAMS FULFILLED

*G*od created us with an overwhelming desire to soar....
He designed us to be tremendously productive and
"to mount up with wings like eagles," realistically
dreaming of what He can do with our potential.

Carol Kent

*T*he human heart, has hidden treasures,
In secret kept, in silence sealed;—
The thoughts, the hopes, the dreams, the pleasures,
Whose charms were broken if revealed.

Charlotte Brontë

I'll lead you to **buried** treasures, secret caches of
valuables—Confirmations that it is, in fact, I, God...
who calls you by your name.

ISAIAH 45:3 THE MESSAGE

DREAMS FULFILLED

THE GIFT OF FAMILY

One of the greatest gifts
That life can give to anyone
Is the very special love that families share...
As years go by,
It's good to know that there will always be
Certain people in our lives who care.

For there are countless things
That only families have in common
And memories that no one else can make...
And these precious ties that bind a family together
Are bonds that time and distance cannot break.

How fortunate we are
When we have relatives to love us,
It makes the world a happy place to be....
Few gifts in life
Will last as long
Or touch the heart as deeply
As the very special gift
Of family.

Craig S. Tunks

Let love and faithfulness never leave you;
bind them around your neck,
write them on the tablet of your heart.

PROVERBS 3:3 NIV

THE GIFT OF FAMILY

_____

_____

_____

_____

_____

_____

_____

_____

_____

_____

_____

_____

_____

_____

_____

HOPE FOR TODAY

*H*ope begins in the dark, the stubborn hope that if you just
show up and try to do the right thing, the dawn will come.
You wait and watch and work: You don't give up.

Anne Lamott

*T*his I call to mind and therefore I have hope: Because of the
Lord's great love we are not consumed, for His compassions never
fail. They are new every morning; great is Your faithfulness.

Lamentations 3:21-23 NCV

*D*o not spoil what you have by desiring what you
have not; but remember that what you now have
was once among the things you only hoped for.

Epicurus

It is difficult to say what is impossible, for the dream of
yesterday is the hope of today and the reality of tomorrow.

ROBERT H. GODDARD

HOPE FOR TODAY

_____

_____

_____

_____

_____

_____

_____

_____

_____

_____

_____

_____

_____

_____

_____

_____

_____

GREAT THINGS

*L*et us examine our capacities and gifts, and then put them to the best use we may. As our own view of life is of necessity partial, I do not find that we can do better than to put them absolutely in God's hands, and look to Him for the direction of our lives.... God can do great things with our lives, if we but give them to Him in sincerity.

Anna R. B. Lindsay

*L*ord, help me do great things as though they were little, since I do them with Your powers; and help me to do little things as though they were great, because I do them in Your Name.

Blaise Pascal

*T*rue worth is in being, not seeming—
In doing, each day that goes by,
Some little good—not in dreaming
Of great things to do by and by.

Alice Cary

**The Lord has done great things for us,
and we are filled with joy.**

PSALM 126:3 NIV

GREAT THINGS

OF GREAT VALUE

*A*re not five sparrows sold for two pennies? Yet not
one of them is forgotten by God. Indeed, the very hairs
of your head are all numbered. Don't be afraid;
you are worth more than many sparrows.

Luke 12:6-7 NIV

*F*or God bought you with a high price.
So you must honor God with your body.

1 Corinthians 6:20 NLT

*F*or you know that it was not with perishable things
such as silver or gold that you were redeemed...
but with the precious blood of Christ.

1 Peter 1:18-19 NIV

You are in the Beloved...therefore infinitely dear
to the Father, unspeakably precious to Him.

NORMAN F. DOWTY

OF GREAT VALUE

_____

_____

_____

_____

_____

_____

_____

_____

_____

_____

_____

_____

_____

_____

_____

_____

_____

PATHS OF LIFE

*But the path of the righteous is like the light of dawn,
that shines brighter and brighter until the full day.*

Proverbs 4:18 NASB

*You have made known to me the paths of life;
You will fill me with joy in Your presence.*

Acts 2:28 NIV

*Thy word is a lamp to my feet
And a light to my path.*

Psalm 119:105 NKJV

*Come, let us go up to the mountain of the Lord.... There He
will teach us His ways, and we will walk in His paths.*

Micah 4:2 NLT

The best things are nearest...light in your eyes,
flowers at your feet, duties at your hand,
the path of God just before you.

ROBERT LOUIS STEVENSON

PATHS OF LIFE

REAL JOY

I've grown to realize the joy that comes from little
victories is preferable to the fun that comes from
ease and the pursuit of pleasure.

Lawana Blackwell

*R*eal joy comes not from ease or riches or from the praise
of men, but from doing something worthwhile.

Sir Wilfred Grenfell

*J*oyful are people of integrity,
who follow the instructions of the Lord.
Joyful are those who obey His laws
and search for Him with all their hearts.

Psalm 119:1-2 NLT

*T*here is no greater joy nor greater reward than to
make a fundamental difference in someone's life.

Mary Rose McGeady

May the God of hope fill you with all joy and peace as you
trust in Him, so that you may overflow with hope.

ROMANS 15:13 NIV

REAL JOY

_____
_____
_____
_____
_____
_____
_____
_____
_____
_____
_____
_____
_____
_____
_____
_____
_____
_____

GOD LISTENS

*O*pen wide the windows of our spirits and fill us full of light;
open wide the door of our hearts, that we may receive and
entertain Thee with all our powers of adoration.

Christina Rossetti

*W*e come this morning—
Like empty pitchers to a full fountain,
With no merits of our own,
O Lord—open up a window of heaven...
And listen this morning.

James Weldon Johnson

*G*od listens in compassion and love, just like we do when
our children come to us. He delights in our presence.

Richard J. Foster

I love the Lord because He hears and answers
my prayers. Because He bends down and listens,
I will pray as long as I have breath!

PSALM 116:1-2 NLT

GOD LISTENS

SHINING THROUGH

*D*on't ever let yourself get so busy that you miss
those little but important extras in life—the beauty of a day...
the smile of a friend...the serenity of a quiet moment alone.
For it is often life's smallest pleasures and gentlest joys
that make the biggest and most lasting difference.

*S*omeone said to me once that we can see the features of God
in a single smile. Look for that smile in the people you meet.

Christopher de Vinck

*D*ear Lord...shine through me, and be so in me that
every soul I come in contact with may feel Your presence
in my soul.... Let me thus praise You in the way
You love best, by shining on those around me.

John Henry Newman

Nothing between us and God, our faces shining with the
brightness of His face...our lives gradually becoming
brighter and more beautiful as God enters our lives.

2 CORINTHIANS 3:18 THE MESSAGE

SHINING THROUGH

ONE HUNDRED YEARS FROM NOW

*W*ise choices will watch over you.
Understanding will keep you safe.

Proverbs 2:11 NLT

*O*ne hundred years from now, it will not matter what my
bank account was, how big my house was, or what kind
of car I drove. But the world may be a little better,
because I was important in the life of a child.

Forest Witcraft

*C*hoices can change our lives profoundly. The choice
to mend a broken relationship, to say yes to a difficult
assignment, to lay aside some important work to
play with a child, to visit some forgotten person—
these small choices may affect our lives eternally.

Gloria Gaither

Half our life is spent trying to find something to do with
the time we have rushed through life trying to save.

WILL ROGERS

ONE HUNDRED YEARS FROM NOW

A STANDARD OF EXCELLENCE

*G*oing far beyond the call of duty, doing more than others expect...is what excellence is all about. And it comes from striving, maintaining the highest standards, looking after the smallest detail, and going the extra mile. Excellence means doing your very best. In everything. In every way.

*T*he highest excellence which an individual can attain must be to work according to the best of his genius and to work in harmony with God's creation.

J. H. Smyth

I studied the lives of great men and famous women, and I found that the men and women who got to the top were those who did the jobs they had in hand with everything they had of energy and enthusiasm and hard work.

Harry S. Truman

Love the Lord God with all your passion and prayer and intelligence and energy.

MARK 12:30 THE MESSAGE

A STANDARD OF
EXCELLENCE

_____

_____

_____

_____

_____

_____

_____

_____

_____

_____

_____

_____

_____

_____

_____

_____

MAKING A DIFFERENCE

Character is like a tree and reputation like its shadow.
The shadow is what we think of it; the tree is the real thing.

Abraham Lincoln

People grow through experience if they meet life honestly
and courageously. This is how character is built.

Eleanor Roosevelt

We can rejoice, too, when we run into problems and trials,
for we know that they help us develop endurance. And endurance
develops strength of character, and character strengthens our
confident hope of salvation. And this hope will not lead to
disappointment. For we know how dearly God loves us, because
He has given us the Holy Spirit to fill our hearts with His love.

Romans 5:3-5 NLT

Character cannot be developed in ease and quiet.
Only through experience of trial and suffering can the soul
be strengthened, ambition inspired, and success achieved.

Helen Keller

Personality can open doors, but only
character can keep them open.

ELMER G. LETTERMAN

MAKING A DIFFERENCE

_____

_____

_____

_____

_____

_____

_____

_____

_____

_____

_____

_____

_____

_____

_____

_____

_____

THE ATTENTION OF GOD

We have been in God's thought from all eternity, and in His creative love, His attention never leaves us.

Michael Quoist

Because God is responsible for our welfare, we are told to cast all our care upon Him, for He cares for us. God says, "I'll take the burden—don't give it a thought—leave it to Me." God is keenly aware that we are dependent upon Him for life's necessities.

Billy Graham

You are God's created beauty and the focus of His affection and delight.

Janet L. Weaver Smith

Give all your worries to Him;
because He cares about you.

1 PETER 5:7 NCV

THE ATTENTION
OF GOD

THE LOVE OF GOD

*C*an anything ever separate us from Christ's love? Does it mean
He no longer loves us if we have trouble or calamity, or are
persecuted, or hungry, or destitute, or in danger, or threatened
with death?... No, despite all these things, overwhelming victory
is ours through Christ, who loved us. And I am convinced that
nothing can ever separate us from God's love. Neither death
nor life, neither angels nor demons, neither our fears for today
nor our worries about tomorrow—not even the powers of
hell can separate us from God's love.

Romans 8:35-36, 38 NLT

Nothing can separate you from His love, absolutely
nothing.... God is enough for time, and God is enough
for eternity. God is enough!

HANNAH WHITALL SMITH

THE LOVE OF GOD

_____
_____
_____
_____
_____
_____
_____
_____
_____
_____
_____
_____
_____
_____
_____
_____
_____
_____

THE GRAND ESSENTIALS

The grand essentials of happiness are: something to do, something to love, and something to hope for.

Allan K. Chalmers

Prayer is essential.... Pray hard and long. Pray for your brothers and sisters. Keep your eyes open. Keep each other's spirits up so that no one falls behind.

Ephesians 6:13 THE MESSAGE

This is the true joy of life, the being used up for a purpose recognized by yourself as a mighty one; being a force of nature instead of a feverish, selfish little clot of ailments and grievances, complaining that the world will not devote itself to making you happy. I am of the opinion that my life belongs to the community, and as long as I live, it is my privilege to do for it what I can.

George Bernard Shaw

Only a **life lived** for others is a **life worthwhile.**

ALBERT EINSTEIN

THE GRAND ESSENTIALS

GOD LOVES YOU

*J*ust as there comes a warm sunbeam into every cottage window, so comes a love-beam of God's care for every separate need.

Nathaniel Hawthorne

*I*t is clear to us, friends, that God not only loves you very much but also has put His hand on you for something special.

1 Thessalonians 1:4 THE MESSAGE

*L*istening to God is a firsthand experience.... God invites *you* to vacation in His splendor. He invites *you* to feel the touch of His hand. He invited *you* to feast at His table. He wants to spend time with *you*.

Max Lucado

Open your hearts to the love God instills....
God loves you tenderly. What He gives you is not
to be kept under lock and key, but to be shared.

MOTHER TERESA

GOD LOVES YOU

LIVE FOR TODAY

We are weaving the future on the loom of today.

Grace Stricker Dawson

*L*ive today! Live fully each moment of today. Trust God to let you work through this moment and the next. He will give you all you need. Don't skip over the painful or confusing moment— even it has its important and rightful place in the day.

*T*oday is unique! It has never occurred before and it will never be repeated. At midnight it will end, quietly, suddenly, totally. Forever. But the hours between now and then are opportunities with eternal possibilities.

Charles R. Swindoll

This is the day the Lord has made.
We will rejoice and be glad in it.

PSALM 118:24 NLT

LIVE FOR TODAY

_____

_____

_____

_____

_____

_____

_____

_____

_____

_____

_____

_____

_____

_____

_____

_____

_____

BLESSINGS

You're blessed when you're content with just who you are—
no more, no less. That's the moment you find yourselves proud
owners of everything that can't be bought. You're blessed when
you've worked up a good appetite for God. He's food and drink
in the best meal you'll ever eat. You're blessed when you care.
At the moment of being "care-full," you find yourselves cared for.
You're blessed when you get your inside world—your mind and
heart—put right. Then you can see God in the outside world.

Matthew 5:5-8 THE MESSAGE

> There is plenitude in God.... God is a vast reservoir
> of blessing who supplies us abundantly.
>
> EUGENE PETERSON

BLESSINGS

IMAGINE ALL YOU CAN

*I*magination is the beginning of creation.
You imagine what you desire, you will what you imagine
and at last you create what you will.

George Bernard Shaw

*L*ook up to the skies.
Who created all these stars?
He leads out the army of heaven one by one
and calls all the stars by name.
Because He is strong and powerful,
not one of them is missing....
Surely you know. Surely you have heard.
The Lord is the God who lives forever,
who created all the world.
He does not become tired or need to rest.
No one can understand how great His wisdom is.
He gives strength to those who are tired
and more power to those who are weak.

Isaiah 40:26, 28–29 NCV

*R*eality can be beaten with enough imagination.

Your imagination, my dear fellow,
is worth more than you imagine.

LOUIS ARAGON

IMAGINE ALL YOU CAN

REMEMBER THAT YOU ARE NEEDED

*N*o love, no friendship can cross the path of our destiny
without leaving some mark on it forever.

A friend loves you all the time, and a brother
helps in time of trouble.

Proverbs 17:17 NCV

*T*here is nothing better than the encouragement of a good friend.

Katharine Butler Hathaway

*B*eing with you is like walking on a very clear morning—
definitely the sensation of belonging there.

E. B. White

Remember that you are needed. There is at least one important
work to be done that will not be done unless you do it.

CHARLES ALLEN

REMEMBER THAT YOU ARE NEEDED

UNIQUE GIFTS

God has a wonderful plan for each person He has chosen.
He knew even before He created this world what beauty
He would bring forth from our lives.

Louis B. Wyly

Everyone has a unique role to fill in the world and is
important in some respect. Everyone, including and
perhaps especially you, is indispensable.

Nathaniel Hawthorne

God gives us all gifts, special abilities that we are entrusted
with developing to help serve Him and serve others.

God has given gifts to each of you from His
great variety of spiritual gifts...so that God's
generosity can flow through you.

1 PETER 4:10 NLT

UNIQUE GIFTS

WIDE OPEN SPACES

*B*y entering through faith into what God has always wanted
to do for us—set us right with Him, make us fit for Him—
we have it all together with God because of our Master Jesus.
And that's not all: We throw open our doors to God and discover
at the same moment that He has already thrown open His
door to us. We find ourselves standing where we always hoped
we might stand—out in the wide open spaces of God's grace
and glory, standing tall and shouting our praise.

Romans 5:1-2 THE MESSAGE

Whoever walks toward God one step,
God runs toward him two.

WIDE OPEN SPACES

BLOOM WHERE YOU ARE PLANTED

*S*o then neither he who plants is anything, nor he who waters, but God who gives the increase. Now he who plants and he who waters are one, and each one will receive his own reward according to his own labor. For we are God's fellow workers.

1 Corinthians 3:7–9 NKJV

*Y*ou wake up in the morning, and lo! your purse is magically filled with twenty-four hours of the magic tissue of the universe of your life. No one can take it from you. No one receives either more or less than you receive. Waste your infinitely precious commodity as much as you will, and the supply will never be withheld from you. Moreover, you cannot draw on the future. Impossible to get into debt. You can only waste the passing movements. You cannot waste tomorrow. It is kept for you.

Arnold Bennett

We are all dreaming of some magical rose garden over the horizon—instead of enjoying the roses that are blooming outside our windows today.

DALE CARNEGIE

BLOOM WHERE YOU ARE PLANTED

_____

_____

_____

_____

_____

_____

_____

_____

_____

_____

_____

_____

_____

_____

_____

_____

_____

EVERY NEED

God wants nothing from us except our needs, and these
furnish Him with room to display His bounty when He
supplies them freely... Not what I have, but what I do not have,
is the first point of contact between my soul and God.

Charles H. Spurgeon

Jesus Christ has brought every need, every joy, every gratitude,
every hope of ours before God. He accompanies us and
brings us into the presence of God.

Dietrich Bonhoeffer

The "air" which our souls need also envelops all of us
at all times and on all sides. God is round about us...
on every hand, with many-sided and all-sufficient grace.

Ole Hallesby

In His unfailing love, my God will stand with me.
He will let me look down in triumph.

PSALM 59:10 NLT

EVERY NEED

_____

_____

_____

_____

_____

_____

_____

_____

_____

_____

_____

_____

_____

_____

_____

_____

_____

_____

_____

MIRACLE OF GRACE

*F*ace your deficiencies and acknowledge them....
Let them teach you patience, sweetness, insight.
When we do the best we can, we never know what miracle
is wrought in our life, or in the life of another.

Helen Keller

*A*ll praise to God, the Father of our Lord Jesus Christ,
who has blessed us with every spiritual blessing in
the heavenly realms because we are united with Christ.

Ephesians 1:3 NLT

*W*here there is faith, there is love.
Where there is love, there is peace.
Where there is peace, there is God.
Where there is God, there is no need.

When the soul has laid down its faults at the feet
of God, it feels as though it had wings.

EUGENIE DE GUERIN

MIRACLE OF GRACE

_____

_____

_____

_____

_____

_____

_____

_____

_____

_____

_____

_____

_____

_____

_____

_____

LIVING LIFE

*B*e aware of wonder. Live a balanced life—learn some and think some and draw and paint and sing and dance and play and work every day some.

Robert Fulghum

*Y*ou have begun to live the new life, in which you are being made new and are becoming like the One who made you. This new life brings you the true knowledge of God.

Colossians 3:10 NCV

*L*ife is about not knowing, having to change, taking the moment and making the best of it, without knowing what's going to happen next. Delicious ambiguity.

Gilda Radner

Here is the test to find whether your mission on Earth
is finished: if you're alive, it isn't.

RICHARD BACH

LIVING LIFE

GOD DELIGHTS IN YOU

*W*e think God's love rises and falls with our performance.
It doesn't.... He loves you for whose you are: you are His child.

Max Lucado

*Y*ou'll get a brand-new name straight from the mouth
of God. You'll be a stunning crown in the palm of God's hand,
a jeweled gold cup held high in the hand of your God.
No more will anyone call you Rejected, and your country
will no more be called Ruined. You'll be called Hephzibah
(My Delight),...because God delights in you.

Isaiah 62:2-5 THE MESSAGE

We are all precious in His sight.

GOD DELIGHTS
IN YOU

_____
_____
_____
_____
_____
_____
_____
_____
_____
_____
_____
_____
_____
_____
_____
_____

THINK ON THESE THINGS

*A*nd now, dear brothers and sisters.... Fix your thoughts on what is true, and honorable, and right, and pure, and lovely, and admirable. Think about things that are excellent and worthy of praise.

Philippians 4:8 nlt

*I*nstead of a gem, or even a flower, we should cast the gift of a lovely thought into the heart of a friend, that would be giving as the angels give.

George MacDonald

*T*he happiness of your life depends upon the character of your thoughts.

The fountain of beauty is the heart, and every generous thought illustrates the walls of your chamber.

FRANCIS QUARLES

THINK ON THESE THINGS

_____

_____

_____

_____

_____

_____

_____

_____

_____

_____

_____

_____

_____

_____

_____

_____

LET THE DAY SUFFICE

*P*eople who don't know God and the way He works fuss over these things, but you know both God and how He works. Steep your life in God-reality, God-initiative, God-provisions. Don't worry about missing out. You'll find all your everyday human concerns will be met.

Matthew 6:32–33 THE MESSAGE

*S*ooner or later we all discover that the important moments in life are not the advertised ones, not the birthdays, the graduations, the weddings, not the great goals achieved. The real milestones are less prepossessing. They come to the door of memory.

Susan B. Anthony

Dance like there's nobody watching
Love like you'll never get hurt
Sing like there's nobody listening
Live like it's heaven on earth
And speak from the heart to be heard.

WILLIAM W. PURKEY

LET THE DAY SUFFICE

FAITHFUL GUIDE

*G*od, who has led you safely on so far, will lead you on to the end. Be altogether at rest in the loving holy confidence which you ought to have in His heavenly Providence.

Francis de Sales

*G*uidance is a sovereign act. Not merely does God...guide us by showing us His way...whatever mistakes we may make, we shall come safely home. Slippings and strayings there will be, no doubt, but the everlasting arms are beneath us; we shall be caught, rescued, restored. This is God's promise; this is how good He is.

J. I. Packer

From now on **every road** you travel
Will take you to God.
Follow the Covenant signs;
Read the charted directions.

PSALM 25:10 THE MESSAGE

FAITHFUL GUIDE

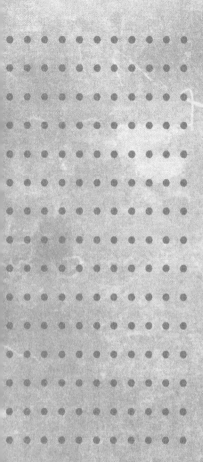

*H*appiness comes of the capacity to feel deeply,
to enjoy simply, to think freely, to risk life, to be needed.

Storm Jameson